Ocean Life

Starfish

By Lloyd G. Douglas

Children's Press®

New York Sydney
g

Photo Credits: Cover © Amos Nachoum/Corbis; p. 5 © Jeffrey L. Rotman/Corbis; p. 7 © Raymond Gehman/Corbis; p. 9 © Fred Whitehead/Animals Animals; p. 11 © Franklin Viola/Animals Animals; p. 13 © Brandon D. Cole/Corbis; p. 15 © George D. Lepp/Corbis; p. 17 © Gray Hardel/Corbis; p. 19 © Zig Leszczynski/Animals Animals or Steve Wrubel/Getty Images, Inc.; p. 21 © Michael Prince/Corbis

Contributing Editor: Shira Laskin
Book Design: Elana Davidian

Library of Congress Cataloging-in-Publication Data

Douglas, Lloyd G.
    Starfish / by Lloyd G. Douglas.
    p. cm. — (Ocean life)
    Includes index.
    ISBN 0-516-25030-2 (lib. bdg.) — ISBN 0-516-23743-8 (pbk.)
    1. Starfishes—Juvenile literature. I. Title.

QL384.A8D68 2005
593.9'3—dc22
                                                    2004010117

Contents

Starfish are not fish.

They are animals with hard, **bumpy** skin.

5

There are many kinds of starfish in the ocean.

They can be different colors and sizes.

Most starfish have five arms.

Some starfish have more than five arms.

If a starfish loses an arm,
it will grow back.

arm growing back

13

Starfish have many small feet on the bottom of their arms.

They are called **tube feet.**

tube feet

15

Starfish use their tube feet to move across the ocean floor.

A starfish's mouth is under its body.

It uses its mouth to eat **clams** and other sea animals.

Some **aquariums** have starfish you can touch.

Go see them for yourself!

New Words

aquariums (uh-**kwair**-ee-uhmz) places you can visit where you can look at many sea animals

bumpy (**buhm**-pee) having many raised, rounded areas

clams (**klamz**) shellfish with two shells that are tightly hinged together and meat inside that can be eaten

starfish (**star**-fish) sea animals that are shaped like stars and have five or more arms

tube feet (**toob feet**) small feet under the arms of the starfish that help it move across the ocean floor

To Find Out More

Books
A Star at the Bottom of the Sea
by Gayle Ridinger
Gareth Stevens Incorporated

Sea Stars
by Lola M. Schaefer
Scholastic Inc.

Web Site
Sea Star: Enchanted Learning Software
http://www.enchantedlearning.com/subjects/invertebrates/
    echinoderm/seastarprintout.shtml
Read about starfish, which are also known as sea stars,
on this Web site.

Index

About the Author
Lloyd G. Douglas writes children's books from his home near the Atlantic Ocean.

Content Consultant
Maria Casas, Marine Research Associate, Graduate School of Oceanography, University of Rhode Island

Reading Consultants
Kris Flynn, Coordinator, Small School District Literacy, The San Diego County Office of Education

Shelly Forys, Certified Reading Recovery Specialist, W.J. Zahnow Elementary School, Waterloo, IL

Paulette Mansell, Certified Reading Recovery Specialist, and Early Literacy Consultant, TX